Understanding The Bowen Technique

Contents

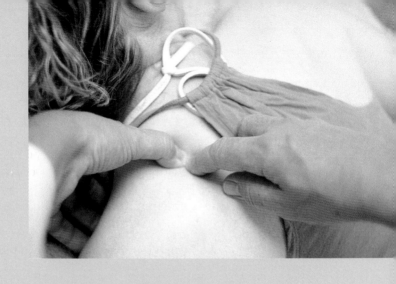

1

Understanding The Bowen Technique

The Bowen Technique is a very gentle form of natural healing. In order to appreciate its subtlety and depth, the therapy really needs to be experienced.

On the face of it, a Bowen session involves only light moves, applied to very specific points on the body, with significant pauses or rests between each series of moves. However, what may not be seen by the casual observer is the dramatic and relaxing effect a Bowen session can have on the whole body.

After their first session people often wonder how such gentle moves can have so powerful an effect – not only on their posture and structural problems (e.g. bad back, frozen shoulder, etc.) but also on their general well-being.

Studies of various 'light touch' therapies have shown that one does not need to use forceful manipulation to achieve significant changes. In fact, it seems that often the lighter the touch, the more effective and profound the effect.

5

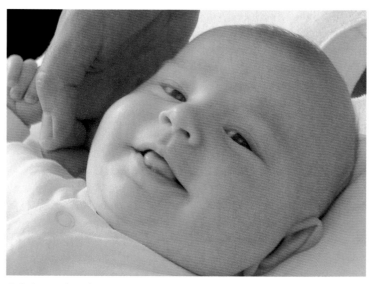

Only the gentlest of touch is used in the Bowen Technique, which makes it suitable for all ages.

The level of touch used in a Bowen session is very gentle, and will vary according to the sensitivity of each client. The therapist uses his fingers or thumbs to move over muscles, ligaments, tendons, fascia and joints (and occasionally directly over nerves themselves), in order to elicit a healing response in the body.

Nothing is imposed from without – the sole intention of the work is to encourage the body to respond by carefully stimulating its own innate ability to heal.

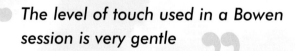

The level of touch used in a Bowen session is very gentle

HOLISTIC HEALING

The Bowen Technique embodies a truly holistic approach to healthcare. It is concerned not just with addressing specific conditions and symptoms, but also with encouraging a natural potential for health to express itself in every aspect of the patient's life.

RELAXATION

A Bowen session is very relaxing. It is mostly performed with the person lying on a treatment table. Tom Bowen (the originator of the work) provided beds in his clinic, in order to encourage a sense of deeper relaxation. Other procedures may be undertaken with the person sitting in a chair or standing up. In fact, it is possible to work in almost any position – in a wheelchair, lying on one's side, or even propped up on one's back. The most important thing for the effectiveness of the session is that the person is comfortable.

TIME OUT

A unique feature of the Bowen Technique is the pause between each series of moves. This is given to allow the body to respond and integrate what is being done. During these pauses, the therapist will usually leave the room. This lets the person relax without feeling that they have to keep up a conversation or that they are being watched.

The pauses vary in duration from person to person and from condition to condition.

Someone who is very sensitive to touch, or someone who has a lot of muscle tightness, may need longer gaps between a series of moves than someone who is relatively supple. A Bowen therapist develops a highly sensitive 'listening touch' that picks up any tensions through the tissues of the body. The therapist can then vary factors, such as touch, pressure and position, depending upon what is required by the client.

2 A Brief History

The Bowen technique was pioneered by a man by the name of Tom Bowen (1916-1982). While he was developing his therapy in Australia in the 1950s and 60s, he was fascinated by the different postures people had, and how this related to their symptoms of ill-health or muscle pain, etc.

Tom Bowen – pioneer of the Bowen Technique.

Tom was a quiet man who did not communicate much of what he was doing. However, he did work closely with some associates, most notably his secretary, Irene Horwood, and Oswald and Elaine Rentsch, whom he entrusted to document his work.

11

HUMBLE BEGINNINGS

Tom grew up in Geelong, Australia, where his parents had moved a few years before his birth. He came from a working-class background and he started his first job as a manual labourer.

There is no doubt that Tom was a natural healer, but he also had an uncanny ability to observe how people walked, sat and moved. He drew remarkably accurate conclusions as to the root cause of their pain.

His fascination with bodywork was born out of a desire to help people who were suffering. He was a deeply religious man and would often say that the development of his therapeutic work was a 'gift of God'.

Tom Bowen did not promote or teach his approach, and he allowed only a very small number of therapists to observe him working. He was dedicated to helping the poor and disenfranchised in the local community, setting up a free clinic for disabled children, working on prisoners in the local penitentiary, and helping out with injuries at the local football club.

ALL GOD'S CREATURES

As well as helping people, Tom had a keen interest in animals, particularly horses. He would frequently be called out to work on farm animals. Nowadays, this work is continued through the efforts of Alison Goward, who developed Equine Muscle Release Therapy (EMRT™)

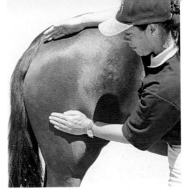

The Bowen Technique is not exclusive to people. A variety of animals can be addressed, including cats, dogs and horses.

and CCMRT™ (Cat and Canine Muscle Release Therapy), which are taught throughout the world.

13

RAPID RESULTS

As a therapist, Tom was incredibly hardworking. A local government survey in 1975 showed him seeing more than 13,000 people a year. He also seemed to get results very quickly. At one time, he asked Oswald Rentsch to get feedback from his clients about their recovery rates. He was amazed by the results. A very high percentage of them reported significant improvements after only a few sessions, even those with quite long-term problems.

Tom had a deep interest in anatomy, and he spent time with some well-known 'manipulators' of his day. However, it is clear that early in his career, his approach took on a whole new dimension and he began working in a radically different way. How this came about, or what instigated it, is difficult to say, but there is no doubt that it was truly inspired.

THE BOWEN TECHNIQUE

The Bowen Technique, as it is taught today, is based on

Oswald Rentsch's interpretation of Tom's work. Bowen developed certain procedures after years of experimentation and clinical trials. It is these procedures that are taught today as the Bowen Technique, Bowenwork® or 'Bowtech'™.

Today's Bowen Technique is based on Oswald Rentsch's interpretation of Tom Bowen's work.

Oswald Rentsch worked with Bowen for many years, refining and documenting the work. However, it was not until 1986 – four years after Tom's death – that the Rentschs began to teach the therapy. Dedicated to preserving the technique and ensuring that it was taught in its original form, they founded the Bowen Therapy Academy of Australia in 1987. Since then, more than 12,000 therapists have been trained worldwide.

15

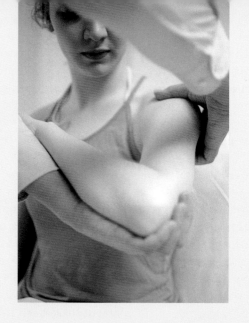

3

How It Works

The Bowen Technique is based on a number of core principles that were observed by its pioneer, Tom Bowen.

FASCIA

Bowen noticed that the body maintained structure through the inter-relationship of key bands of muscle via what is known as fascia. You may have noticed white, translucent sheets of very tough tissue when preparing meat – this is fascia.

Fascia consists of tough sheets (sometimes tubes) of connective tissue, which provide coverings of variable strength and thickness for every structure in the body. All muscles are surrounded by it. It allows flexibility and movement between the various parts of the body.

One function of these bands of fascia is to maintain upright posture. Consequently, fascia receives a lot of attention in a Bowen session, as it has such a profound effect on posture and, in particular, the way we hold our spine.

Structural bands of fascia are vitally important in maintaining upright posture. Here we can see how fascia is involved in the process of the baby going from crawling to standing.

Imagine that your spine is a tent pole, being held in position by guy ropes (in this case the bands of fascia that support the back). It is easy to see how undue tension or weakness in any one of these might cause a bend or create tension in the pole. Such an effect on the spine could result in reactions, such as pressure on nerves as they exit the spinal column, tension in the musculature on one side of the body, and compensation patterns being set up in the rest of the body.

Some complementary therapies manipulate the spine to address the relationship between individual bones (for example, to free a trapped nerve). In contrast, a Bowen session addresses the muscle and fascial relationships that are holding the spine in that particular position. By changing the way in which the muscles and fascia relate to each other, a change in structure becomes inevitable, forcing the spine to adopt a better position. This approach usually has a longer lasting effect.

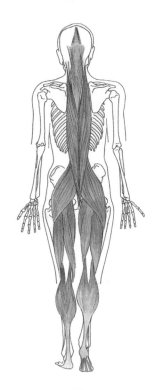

The continuity of muscles up the back and down the legs means that this relationship is given a lot of attention in Bowen sessions. Manipulation of these muscles can have a profound effect on the spine and posture.

THE BOWEN MOVE

A classic Bowen move over a muscle or tendon consists of the therapist's fingers or thumbs being placed on the body (or on light clothing). The skin is drawn lightly away, and a gentle challenge (push) is made on the muscle or tendon. This challenge is held for a few seconds before a

Bowen moves can be performed through light clothing.

'rolling' move is made over the muscle itself. The action of this type of move elicits a powerful effect on the body on a number of levels, not just the musculo-skeletal system.

Tom Bowen used his own language to explain what he was doing. For example, he would describe how some of these moves would act as 'stoppers', to contain and amplify the effect of the work in areas of the body that needed attention. Other hand positions would act as 'holding points', to divert energetic impulses created by the move and to enable him to feel responses as he worked.

THE BRAIN AND NERVES

One way of explaining how the technique works is to look at its effect on the nerves within muscles. Firstly, as a challenge is placed on a muscle and the muscle is gently stretched, the stretch receptors (which lie alongside muscle fibres inside the muscle) begin to send sensory information along the nerve pathways to the spinal cord. There are many thousands of stretch receptors or muscle spindles in each muscle (approximately 7-30 per gram of muscle tissue). Thousands of times in each second, they send information to the brain about the status of individual muscles.

During a session, a stretch on the muscle is maintained for several seconds before the move itself is made. During and after the move, further sensory information is sent via nerves to the spinal cord and then to various areas of the brain. A similar procedure occurs when working on tendons, although the sensory nerves in tendons are sensitive to resistance rather than to stretch, and a slightly slower and firmer pressure is used when moving over these.

After the sensory information induced by the Bowen move reaches the spinal cord, it passes through the nerve pathways to different centres of the brain. Here, the information is shunted backwards and forwards via a complex, self-corrective feedback mechanism. Following this, information is sent back down the spinal cord to individual muscles.

When we are awake and moving around, positional information from our muscles, tendons, joints, skin and fascia is being processed by the brain. While we are lying down, there is very little activity happening within this self-corrective system. For an effective session, it is essential that there is as little interference as possible from the conscious part of the brain (our cortex) or from our muscles, so that this feedback mechanism can re-orient without disturbance.

Bowen moves are made at key structural points in the body, which the brain uses as natural reference points to determine the body's posture. As a result, certain Bowen moves have a profound effect on the way that the body holds itself.

BOWEN PRINCIPLES

While the basic principles behind the Bowen Technique are relatively straightforward, there are a number of factors that can greatly influence the effectiveness of the therapy:

- If a Bowen therapist were to do many extraneous moves without pauses, the effect would be greatly minimized. This is why a favourite Bowen maxim is 'less is more'.
- If the person is not relaxed or comfortable, the primitive areas of the brain that are involved with the co-ordination of movement would not be able to 'hear' and process this distinct information to its benefit. It would be a bit like someone trying to listen to precise

instructions while a hammer drill was being used in the background.

- Certain clinical situations can greatly enhance a Bowen session. For example, it is more conducive to relaxation if the room is warm, as cold temperature actually alerts the brain. It is essential that the person feels safe, that there is no harsh lighting, and that conversation, if any, is limited to observations of physical sensation that might be occurring.

ALTERNATIVE EXPLANATIONS

There are many other explanations as to how the Bowen Technique works. For example, it is clear that some of the points addressed relate to acupuncture meridians and trigger points.

RECENT RESEARCH

Many therapists have noticed a response through their hands as they work, as though an electrical impulse were created as a result of a move. Tom Bowen used to describe how he took the information from these subtle impulses to read responses in the body as he was working.

In fact, these impulses are scientifically recordable. It has been shown that the creation of a stretch in the fascia does indeed initiate a small electrical charge. Studies in the USA have identified them as being created by the tiny collagen fibres that make up the bulk of fascia. It has also been established that these impulses have powerful healing effects on the body.

Experiments have shown that passing a low-level current of this type over a broken bone will greatly speed up repair.

There has been much research in recent years into the complex communication systems arising from the interplay between the body's tissues and fluids. Already, researchers have noticed changes in the constitution of blood on a cellular level after a Bowen session. As more research is published, it will no doubt shed more light on how the Bowen Technique works.

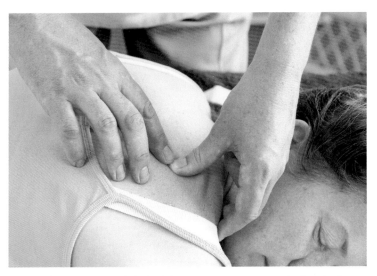

A skilled therapist can 'read' the body's response to a session and adjust the Bowen moves accordingly.

4 Posture

Posture is a major influencing factor in the origin of our physical aches and pains.

COMPENSATION

Our bodies are incredibly resilient at absorbing and dealing with the physical and emotional knocks that life throws at us. When we face a problem – either physical or mental – we develop coping strategies as a response.

These complex compensation patterns enable us to maintain balance and order in our lives. However, these patterns can have a physical cost (and frequently an emotional cost, too).

If someone has experienced a car accident that has involved a blow to their pelvis, it is likely that this will be reflected in every other part of their body – from the feet right up to the neck and shoulders. You might notice that, for example, a high hip on one side of the body may be reflected in a high shoulder on the other side.

A common posture in our

culture involves the head coming forward in relation to the rest of the body. An inevitable result of this is that the hips will come forward in compensation, and the chest becomes depressed and tight, restricting breathing. This can have a cascade of physical and emotional effects.

What is interesting to observe is the way in which tight and weak areas of the body compensate for each other, in order to to allow us to maintain balance. These relationships often change dramatically after a Bowen session. It is not simply the case that tight muscles 'let go' (although that does happen), but rather that relationships between the structural holding patterns change.

NON-PHYSICAL EFFECTS ON POSTURE

Sometimes, postural problems can relate to unconscious psychological or emotional states. The posture shown opposite is reminiscent of a primitive startle reflex that all mammals display when under

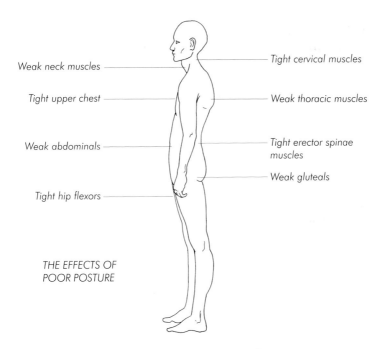

Weak neck muscles

Tight upper chest

Weak abdominals

Tight hip flexors

Tight cervical muscles

Weak thoracic muscles

Tight erector spinae muscles

Weak gluteals

THE EFFECTS OF POOR POSTURE

stress. This is a protective mechanism, which was probably very useful when we were startled by a sabre-toothed tiger, but is less useful today when we are dealing with our line manager demanding more productivity!

BOWEN EFFECTS
Bowen therapists sometimes talk about the different effects on posture, particularly 'ascending' and 'descending' influences. The key to an effective session is to find where the original organizing factor in someone's condition is located. For example, a knee injury might be due to a weak toe joint or a pelvic imbalance that is putting undue strain on the knee as that person walks. Similarly, headaches may be the result of an old fall on the tailbone.

There are many factors involved that affect posture; birth, dental work and even whether a baby is bottle- or breast-fed can have a profound effect on posture later in life. It is crucial to the effectiveness of the session

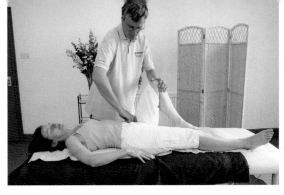

The Bowen Technique can have a dramatic effect on posture. Here the therapist is working on the pelvic area, to allow areas that are overcompensating to 'reset' correctly.

that the root cause of a condition is addressed. Unless this happens, the person's symptoms are likely to return.

One of the interesting things to observe is the ability of the body to process old accidents during and after the session. It is almost as if the body stores a 'memory' of a blow or trauma, which can be held in a frozen state for many years. Bowen work seems to allow the body to 'unfreeze' those areas that have been compensating ever since.

5

Applications

Bowen therapists often have particular areas of expertise.

Some therapists might work with sports injuries, some will concentrate on musculo-skeletal problems (back pain, frozen shoulders, whiplash injuries, etc.) while others might specialise in working with mothers, babies, those in palliative care, or the long-term chronically ill. It is worth asking a therapist what experience they have in working with your type of condition.

Most therapists have a particular area of expertise. The knee work being practiced here is typical of moves used to address sports injuries.

RESEARCH FINDINGS

A research study on the effectiveness of the Bowen Technique in addressing a frozen shoulder was undertaken by the University of Central Lancashire. It showed that, after only a few sessions, sufferers showed significantly improved mobility and pain reduction.

Other research projects underway on the Bowen Technique include dealing with pelvic pain during and after pregnancy, and in recovery rates post-mastectomy.

THERAPY SUCCESS

The technique has a very good record in addressing the conditions listed on page 38. Bear in mind, however, that success varies from person to person – a Bowen therapist is addressing the person as a whole, not just the condition.

One of the most noticeable effects of a Bowen session is the feeling of well-being that it induces. This is believed to be due to the powerful effect the Bowen Technique has on the autonomic (self-regulating) nervous system.

For many of us, stress is a constant factor in our lives. Long-term stress can lead to hyperactivity in our nervous system. This can wreak havoc with our immune system, sleeping patterns, digestion and many other aspects of our health. Just allowing our nervous system to slow down during a Bowen session can have a beneficial effect on all aspects of our being.

> *One of the most noticeable effects of a Bowen session is the feeling of well-being that it induces*

CONDITIONS THAT CAN BE ADDRESSED WITH THE BOWEN TECHNIQUE

- Anxiety/stress-related conditions
- Back pain, sciatica and spinal problems
- Newborn baby problems (e.g. colic, feeding problems and sleep-related conditions)
- Digestive and bowel problems (such as irritable bowel syndrome)
- Fibromyalgia, chronic fatigue syndrome and ME (Myalgic Encephalopathy)
- General muscle stiffness
- Gynaecological conditions (such as heavy or painful periods, infertility and fibroids)
- Headaches and migraines
- Hormonal imbalances
- Joint problems (such as tennis elbow, frozen shoulder, ankle and knee injuries)
- Post-dental trauma, temporo-mandibular joint problems and jaw disorders
- Post-operative recovery
- Respiratory conditions
- Repetitive strain injuries and carpal tunnel syndrome
- Sports injuries
- Whiplash injuries
- Blood pressure (high or low)
- Respiratory problems (such as asthma)

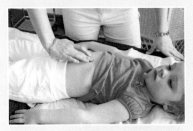

Working on the diaphragm can help with respiratory problems, such as asthma.

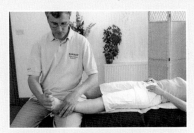

Gentle work around the ankle can assist repair after a sprain.

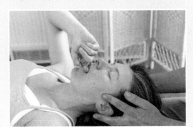

Placing a finger in the mouth when addressing jaw problems allows access to the joint.

Even whiplash injuries can be addressed – using only the gentlest of moves.

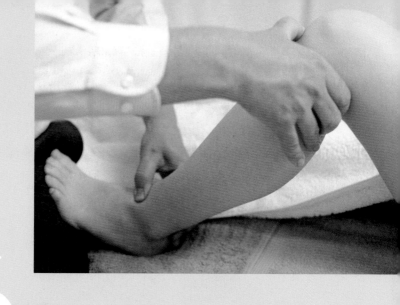

6 A Bowen Session

A Bowen session will involve a number of elements, beginning with a detailed case history.

CASE HISTORY

It is important that you provide as full a picture as possible, covering medication, operations, accidents or falls. All information is confidential. The more information you give – not just about symptoms, but also about lifestyle, exercise, diet and general well-being – the easier it is to tailor the session.

SILENCE IS GOLDEN

Bowen moves work best if the session is carried out without conversation, so that the brain is not distracted. However, it is important to let the therapist know if any unusual sensations are experienced, as this will affect the session.

SENSORY PERCEPTION

It is quite common for people to feel mild sensations of heat, tingling, numbness, cold, changed emotions or a whole host of other experiences during a session. One person

It is not uncommon for clients to experience a range of sensations during a session. Most common is a powerful feeling of deep calm and relaxation.

42

may feel warmth in an area of the back that has been troubling them. Another who has an unbalanced posture may feel as if their leg is lengthening slightly. Such reactions are common, and are nearly always associated with a deep sense of relief and letting go.

THE GENTLE TOUCH
The touch used in the proper application of Tom Bowen's work is always gentle – nothing that could be painful or uncomfortable is ever done. Indeed, too heavy a touch can negate the value of the move because the brain will process the message differently. It is so non-invasive that it is not uncommon for clients to fall asleep during treatment.

Treatment can be performed through light clothing and permission is sought before undertaking any hands-on contact.

Where practitioners work around sensitive areas of the body (close to the groin, for example), particular caution is taken to ensure that the person feels comfortable and

The therapist will always ask permission if there is a need to adjust clothing.

Work around the groin area is carefully negotiated.

Babies and children are handled very sensitively, with parents or guardians present throughout the session.

understands what is being done and why.

Practitioners are trained to exercise deep sensitivity in cases where there may be a history of abuse.

When addressing babies, children and teenagers, practitioners encourage a parent or chaperone to be present.

Bowen moves are usually performed on the left side of the body first.

WATER

Many people are chronically dehydrated due to their lifestyle (e.g. drinking tea, coffee and alcohol, living in centrally heated houses, or taking little exercise). For the average adult, an intake of between 1.5 and 2 litres (50-75 ounces or 2-3.5 pints) of water per day is recommended.

In some cases, people have high levels of toxins in the body. This could be from a build-up of lactic acid in the muscles through too much exercise, or as a result of toxins

45

Applying the kidney procedure can help with the elimination of toxins.

created by drinking, smoking, or recreational drug use. In cases such as these, practitioners may advise drinking distilled water for a short while after a session. Distilled water is essentially very pure. There are very little, if any, trace minerals in it, so it helps to get rid of unwanted toxins.

Drinking water can be very important in situations where there is slight muscle stiffness or mild flu-like symptoms for 24 hours after the session. This is a sign that the body is trying to detoxify. Giving it a helping hand by drinking water and not sitting still for too long greatly helps in this process.

DIET
A Bowen therapist will not normally recommend a change in diet, unless he or she is a qualified nutritionist. However, Tom Bowen was very

interested in naturopathic approaches to health.

His own wife suffered badly from asthma, and he found that certain changes to her diet seemed to help (omitting dairy products, for example). Similarly, avoiding dairy and gluten products can have a huge impact on child behavioural problems (e.g. ADDHD and autism). Your therapist may suggest a visit to a nutritional expert.

ENVIRONMENT

Bowen therapists will look at possible environmental effects on health. For example, a child's respiratory problems may be due to exposure to aerosol sprays or animals (cats are particularly implicated). Changing a pillow or avoiding cut flowers often makes a big difference to asthmatics.

EXERCISE

Exercise can be an important factor in recovery. Too much can result in re-injury. Too little can lead to stasis, tissue adhesions, and an inability for the lymphatic system (the system that keeps our body tissues clean and healthy) to operate effectively.

A gentle exercise regime is the best solution, such as walking about 20 minutes a day, combined with specific exercises for the back or shoulders. Many Bowen therapists have good working relationships with local exercise teachers (Yoga, Pilates, etc.) and will suggest some sessions with them to establish a safe and effective regime – others may recommend a visit to a nutritionist or homoeopath.

CONTRAINDICATIONS

There are a number of factors that seem to interfere with the effectiveness of a Bowen session. Exposure to extremes of temperature is one. This would include having a long, hot bath or putting a hot water bottle or an ice-pack on an area that has been addressed.

Other forms of complementary therapy (particularly manipulative forms, such as chiropractic, osteopathy, massage and acupuncture) should not be undertaken within a week before or after a Bowen session. The Bowen Technique is very subtle, so the work needs to be 'nursed' a little in the days after the session.

During this time, the body is still responding to and integrating the moves. Drinking plenty of water, taking moderate exercise, and avoiding extremes of movement will all help in this process of recovery and repair.

MOTHERS AND BABIES

Tom Bowen developed an approach to helping women during the later stages of pregnancy, especially those experiencing back pain or sciatica. Today, many women have reported that the technique greatly eases labour and delivery. It also has a good record in helping couples who are having difficulty conceiving.

For the baby, symptoms such as colic and restlessness can be helped by Bowen. Usually, only one or two sessions are required. If the baby has had a difficult birth (e.g. Caesarean or ventouse delivery), gentle work around the head and neck can also help.

7 Frequently Asked Questions

The following questions are among the most common queries that new clients of the Bowen Technique tend to ask.

How do I know if a practitioner is qualified?

Practitioners current in their registration with the Bowen Therapy Academy of Australia are listed on the international website directories www.bowtech.com or www.bowenwork.com.

Training courses consist of a number of practical and written assessments, as well as a complete set of coursework.

Many practitioners are already physiotherapists or osteopaths, while others come from a background in sports massage, reflexology or healing.

What is the normal interval between sessions?

Sessions last between 30 and 45 minutes, and, ideally, take place approximately 5 to 10 days apart. Although people often notice significant benefits after just one session, most

The Bowen Technique is so gentle that it is not uncommon for clients to fall asleep during a session!

therapists will recommend further sessions. Some chronic conditions may require ongoing, long-term sessions.

How safe is the Bowen Technique?

The Bowen Technique uses such a gentle level of touch that it is considered to be one of the safest of therapies. This gentleness means that it is ideal for use on people of all ages – from newborns through to the elderly – with all manner of problems.

There are only a small number of cases where

caution must be observed.
These include:

- Pregnancy
- People who have implants
  (such as breast implants)
- After operations on the jaw
  and temporo-mandibular
  joint.

How much does it cost?
Prices of Bowen sessions vary
depending on location and the
credentials of the practitioner.
However, you can expect to
pay a similar figure as for
massage or other bodywork in
your area, and sometimes less

*There are only a small number of
conditions that the Bowen Technique
cannot address, but particular care
must be taken when working with the
temporo-mandibular joint.*

if the practitioner is set up to
address multiple clients at
once.

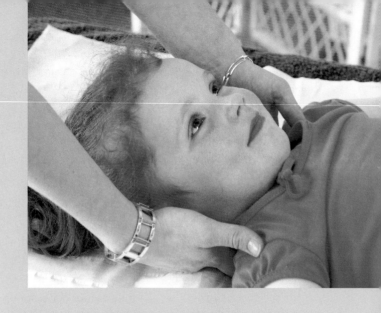

8

Case Histories

The following case histories illustrate how the Bowen Technique can be successfully applied to a number of common problems.

❶ BACK PAIN

A retired builder of 67, Kevin had a long-standing back problem. He'd slipped a disc five years ago and had made a partial recovery, but he was experiencing sciatic pain down his left leg, which was interfering with his sleep.

On assessment, it was clear that he had restricted movement around his sacro-iliac joint at the base of his spine, probably caused by many years of lifting and carrying. He responded well to the first session, where the therapist only worked on his lower back. He reported a significant reduction in pain levels after 24 hours.

At the second session, the therapist worked around his

pelvis and hips to ease the pressure on the sciatic nerve, and addressed the upper back and neck. By the fourth visit, he reported being pain-free. He was given a series of exercises to ensure that his back remained flexible.

❷ FIBROMYALGIA

Sheila had suffered from fibromyalgia for three years. Every fibre in her body was sensitive, and she was finding it difficult to sleep. Her inability to work due to her condition was making her depressed.

The therapist took some time to explain various self-help strategies, including dietary and exercise regimes that might help her condition. Very little physical work was carried out at the first session.

On her return, Sheila admitted that she had been dubious about the technique after the first session, but had noticed a marked reduction in her pain levels. Her sleep seemed marginally improved.

At the second session, the therapist was able to do more work.

When Sheila returned for the third session, she reported a significant increase in her energy levels, and her pain had decreased to the extent that she was considering going back to work.

Over the following months, Sheila found that having regular sessions every three weeks allowed her to lead a relatively normal life. Her whole outlook took on a more positive slant, and she felt more able to deal with her condition on a daily basis.

❸ COLIC AND NEWBORN PROBLEMS

The start of Kylie's life had been anything but easy. After a 24-hour labour, her mother had to undergo an emergency Caesarean section. Kylie was brought in for a session at four months of age, suffering from severe colic and sleep problems.

The therapist noticed some tightness around Kylie's

diaphragm and compression in her neck. At the first session, the therapist worked very gently around Kylie's tummy.

When Kylie returned a week later, both parents remarked on how much more content Kylie seemed to be. Her colic was around 50 per cent improved.

This session and the subsequent session, the therapist worked around Kylie's neck. By the third session, the parents were so happy with Kylie's progress that the therapist advised only coming again for a session if they felt Kylie needed it.

❹ CRUCIATE LIGAMENT PROBLEMS IN THE KNEE

Christopher was a professional athlete. During a training session, he had suffered damage to the anterior cruciate ligament in his knee. This had resulted in considerable swelling and pain.

On Christopher's first visit, it was possible to perform

only the lightest of moves, due to the swelling. The therapist put a support bandage on his ankle, which had also suffered a sprain. He advised application of a washing soda pack that night to draw off some of the fluids.

The Bowen Technique is ideal for athletes suffering from sport-related injuries, such as knee sprain.

Despite minimal work at the first session, Christopher noticed a considerable easing of symptoms during the first week, and a reduction in the swelling.

The therapist performed more detailed work around Christopher's knee and ankle at the second session. After a few days, Christopher telephoned to say that he was now able to resume full training, that the swelling had disappeared completely, and that, on a scale of one to ten, his discomfort was down to one.

Further information

Bowen Associations throughout the world and the Bowenwork Academy USA keep registers of qualified Bowenwork therapists. They are all graduates of the Bowen Therapy Academy of Australia, have a current first-aid certificate and are active in continuing professional development.

To find a practitioner in the UK, contact the Bowen Association of the UK: Tel: 0700 269 8324 or visit www.bowen-technique.co.uk
For training in the UK call 0700 269 3685 or see www.bowentraining.co.uk

To find a practitioner in the USA, or for information about training, contact Bowenwork Academy USA:
Tel: 1-866-862-6936 or visit www.bowenworkacademyusa.com
or: www.bowtech.com

For enquiries outside the USA, please contact: The Bowen Therapy Academy of Australia,
PO Box 733, Hamilton,
3300 Victoria, Australia.
Tel (03) 5572 3000
Web: www.bowtech.com

Individual country's offices are listed online at www.bowtech.com or www.bowenwork.com

The Bowen Association is a member of the Bowen Forum, a body formed in conjunction with other Bowen practitioner organisations in the UK to oversee the establishment of National Occupational Standards and a single regulatory body for the profession.

For details about the Bowen Forum, see www.cnhc.org.uk or www.bowenforum.org.uk

For information about Bowen on horses and small animals, see www.emrt.net.au.

TRAINING

Training for the Bowen Technique is detailed and gives support to existing therapists through advanced courses.

Courses normally last around nine months. Provision is made for those who have not had previous bodywork training. For information on what to look for in a training course, consult *Choosing a Course in Complementary Healthcare, A Student Guide,* published by the Prince of Wales's Foundation for Integrated Health. It is available online at www.fihealth.org.uk

For details of courses available, please contact the Bowen Association of the UK.

FURTHER READING

The Bowen Technique
Author: Julian Baker
Publisher: Corpus Publishing Limited.

The Bowen Technique – the inside story
Author: John Wilks
Publisher: CYMA Limited.

Applying the Bowen Technique (DVD)
Author: John Wilks
Publisher: CYMA Limited.

About the author

John Wilks practises the Bowen Technique in Dorset and Somerset. He is the former chair of the Bowen Association of the UK and is a senior instructor for the Bowen Therapy Academy of Australia. Since 1999, he has taught the Bowen Technique in the UK, Ireland, Belgium, Greece, Australia, USA, Israel, Denmark, Sweden, Norway and Kuwait. He is also author of *Understanding Craniosacral Therapy*, published in the same series by First Stone Publishing, and *The Bowen Technique – the inside story* published by CYMA Ltd.

"John Wilks' comprehensive and compelling work is essential reading for healthcare professionals and those with an interest in this fascinating technique. I have much pleasure in fully endorsing this publication."
Oswald Rentsch, Director, Bowen Academy of Australia.

ACKNOWLEDGEMENTS
Thanks are due to Ellen Cobb, Nicola Hok, Alastair McLoughlin, Oswald and Elaine Rentsch, Rosemary Gordon, Alison Redman, The Grove Neighbourhood Centre, Kenny Kilmurray, Sarah Bernsen, Emma Deegan, Alison Goward, Alexia Monroe and Scott Wurtz. Special thanks to Naren Wilks (www.naren.co.uk) for photography, and Daniela B Larsen for modelling.

Other titles in the series

First published in 2004 by First Stone Publishing
The Old Hen House, St Martin's Farm, Zeals, Warminster, BA12 6NZ.

This edition published in 2009, reprinted in 2011 and 2014 by First Stone Publishing

The contents of this book are for information only and are not intended as a substitute for appropriate medical attention. The author and publishers admit no liability for any consequences arising from following any advice contained within this book. If you have any concerns about your health or medication, always consult your doctor.

ISBN 1 904439 36 5

Printed by Printworks Global Ltd. London & Hong Kong